Overcome Your Obstacles - Increase Your Focus - Improve Your Results

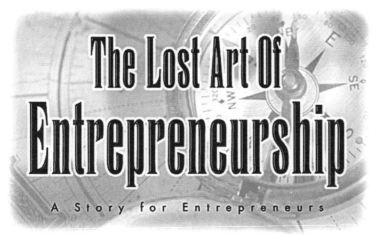

The Lost Art Of Entrepreneurship

A Story for Entrepreneurs

Rediscovering The Principles That Will Guarantee Your Success

Melvin J. Gravely II, Ph.D.

Edited by Shirley Allen
Cover design and inside layout by Ad Graphics, Inc., Tulsa, OK

Gravely, II, Melvin J.,
The Lost Art Of Entrepreneurship:
Rediscovering The Principles That Will Guarantee Your Success

ISBN 0-9656194-5-1

Mailing address:
Impact Group Consultants Publisher
P.O. Box 62126, Cincinnati, OH 45262-2126

Other Books by *Mel Gravely*

Making It Your Business
The Personal Transition From Employee To Entrepreneur

Grandma's Greatest Gifts
Lessons They Shared by Living

DEDICATION

To my parents,

Sarah Gravely and Melvin Gravely, Sr.

Thank you for showing me the value of hard work,
determination, and, most of all, the
"lost art" of principles.

ACKNOWLEDGMENTS

Books do not just happen. The efforts of the author are obvious but, in my case, many others played a significant role in *The Lost Art Of Entrepreneurship*. Thank you all for your patience, opinions, and prayers.

My wife Chandra. You were the first to read this work and your input inspired me.

My editor Shirley Allen. You really are great.

My Master Mind Group Members, Otis Williams and Tammy Wynn. Your constant support, review and input added more value than you will ever know. Thank you.

To the group of peers who reviewed and provided insight to this work, I am blessed to have such great friends in my life. Thank you all:

Angie Avery, Cliff Bailey, Mike Duncan, Joan Fox, Vanessa Freytag, Jewel Grafton, Judy Clark Harris, Modena Henderson, Patti Holmes, Arlene Koth, Lyn Marsteller, Sandra Tally, Clara Villarosa, John Wagner, and John Webb.

THE LOST ART OF ENTREPRENEURSHIP

"...his obstacles were just as real to him as mine are to me."

CHAPTER
1

THE GATHERING

What Are Friends For?

When Joan arrived, John and Cliff were already there. She did not see Patti but Joan was sure she was on her way. The group of business owners had been getting together four to five times a year for the last few years and Patti was always late.

The group started out as strictly business. Their purpose was to share ideas, talk about new approaches and discuss challenges. It did not take long for the relationships to become much more than just business. They were friends, and although they still discussed many business matters, they came together most of all to support one another.

As Joan approached the large table for six in the middle of the restaurant she could not help smiling. She always looked forward to these meetings. When she was a few steps away, John and Cliff both rose to greet her. They exchanged hugs and kisses and sat down.

After a few minutes of friendly banter John asked, "Joan, have you read the book, *The Lost Art Of Entrepreneurship?*" He already knew the answer. Joan was the group's most avid reader. She often recommended books for the members of the group to read. "You know I have, John," she replied. "I read everything I can get my hands on about entrepreneurship."

"Then tell us, oh wise one, what did you think?" John joked.

Joan smiled at John's attempt at humor and replied, "In a word, guys, the book was great. However, I must admit that I had my doubts at the beginning. The first few pages made me think it was going to be one of those 'somebody done me wrong songs.'"

Cliff looked puzzled, "What do you mean?"

"Well, Fenton almost immediately starts talking about his obstacles."

"Who's Fenton?" Cliff asked.

"He's the main character in the story" John replied.

"He was talking about how the system was holding him back. All of his problems were someone else's fault. You know. You've heard it before." Joan concluded.

"I'm glad you said that, because I thought the same thing," John added. "But as I read on I got it."

"Got what?" asked Cliff.

"I got the fact that Fenton faced obstacles that represented the obstacles we all face. And although I did not necessarily understand all of his obstacles, they were just as real to him as mine are to me."

Joan nodded her head in agreement.

John continued, "But you know, even before I read the first few pages I was skeptical. I thought, 'how can this simple short story teach me anything meaningful about business?' But man, was I wrong."

Joan interrupted, "You guys know that I read a lot of books, but this one was really different."

"What do you mean 'different'?" Cliff asked.

"I mean the lessons in this book changed my business." Joan paused, rolling her eyes upward to collect her thoughts. "I read the book a little over a month ago. It led me to make some subtle but valuable changes in my business, and we are already seeing the results of what we've done. The story just pulls you in and actually makes the lessons more relevant."

"I agree," nodded John as he took a drink from his diet cola.

Cliff just listened. He was not much of a reader but he was always interested in the insight the others got from books.

"So, if this book was so great, what did it teach you?" Cliff asked.

"On no, not this time, Cliff. There is no reason you can't read this book. In a little over an hour you can get your own lesson first hand this time." Joan said smiling.

John saw Patti come through the door of the restaurant. "Here comes Patti," he said.

Patti started to asked the hostess where her group was seated but saw them waving their hands. Wearing her usual smile, she approached the table.

Everyone stood to exchange greetings and then sat down.

"OK, guys, what did I miss?" Patti asked.

"If you have not read *The Lost Art Of Entrepreneurship*, it appears you have missed a lot." Cliff said sarcastically.

"Oh you guys read it too?" Patti asked.

"Joan and I have read it," John said.

"I just read it on my plane ride back from Dallas" Patti explained.

"Patti, what did you think of it?"

"Well, I don't want to say much because I don't want to ruin the story for Cliff." She looked a bit disheveled as she fumbled through her briefcase. Finally, she pulled out three books and placed them on the table. "But let me just say that I thought enough of the book to stop by the bookstore at the airport and buy each of you one." She handed each of them their copy.

Patti leaned forward. Her expression was serious. "Guys, it is clear to me that if we are going to really succeed in business, we have to know the principles that are in this book."

Each person thanked Patti for her thoughtfulness and the group went on to talk about Patti's trip to Dallas, Joan's new employee and John's product pricing issues. But Cliff was no longer listening. He opened the book to the first page and began to read.

*"The obstacles don't have
to stop you."*

CHAPTER
2

THE LETTER

Why Didn't They Just Call?

A package was sitting in the center of his desk, which Fenton thought he had cleared before he left the afternoon before. He picked up the thin cardboard overnight mail envelope. It was from the bank and addressed to him. *What is this?*, he wondered. Without even taking off his jacket he sat down in his chair. The bank had never before sent mail to him like this. It had to be serious. He took a deep breath and began to open the package. He pulled out the one page letter.

"Dear Mr. Rice, After careful analysis of your latest financial statements and your loan payment history, we are concerned about your company's performance. After three years of strong performance, this is the second consecutive year your company has failed to meet its objectives. We wish to review your financial statements again at the end of the year. We hope this will give you time to begin to show significant improvement. We will be forced to take more aggressive action to secure our outstanding loans with your company if your performance has not improved at that time."

The letter continued with the standard business letter closing and was signed by Robert Case.

Fenton could not remember being this angry. He was livid. This is just another example of the system out to get black businesses. The bank would never talk this way to a white guy! They say they want our business and then when they get it, this is how they treat us.

As Fenton put the letter back, he noticed a handwritten note in the bottom of the envelope. It was from his banker Carol.

What could she have to say? Fenton thought.

> "Fenton, I'm sorry that this letter is so strong but this matter is serious. My boss is all over me about the late payments and a business that is not performing. I want to work with you, but you have to give me something to work with. I still have confidence in you. Let me know how I can help. Sincerely, Carol S."

"Sure, she wants to help. That sister has been brain washed. She is as bad as they are," he said aloud.

The ring of the telephone startled Fenton. It was too early for customers and he wondered who could be calling.

"Fenton Rice Marketing Group."

"Fenton Rice, please." a smooth female voice asked.

Fenton would recognize that voice anywhere.

"This is he."

"Fenton, this is Carol from the bank."

What is it now? Fenton thought. "How can I help you, Carol?"

"I can tell from your tone that you got the letter from Bob."

"Yes, I did."

"I apologize, but that's Bob's style and this matter is serious."

"Yes, I read your note. Tell me, Carol, why didn't you warn me this was coming?"

"What do you mean? We've talked about your company's performance every month or so for the last year and a half."

"Carol, I thought you were different. I really thought you were in our corner. You're no better than they are."

"Hold on, Fenton. You're singing that song to the wrong audience. This is Carol. I know you. You keep suggesting that this is about race and maybe it is but what you seem to miss is that every entrepreneur has obstacles. The bottom line is, no matter the other issues, you are not getting it done. You know as well as I do that I have been there with you every step of the way. You just haven't been hearing me."

Carol and Fenton had been friends before she was his banker. She was right. She had warned that things were off track. She had made suggestions for improvement. But Fenton really didn't want to hear any of it. He knew what he was doing. Besides, he knew of others who were worse off and the bank kept giving them more money.

Fenton asked, not wanting to stop being mad, "Carol, if you guys have all the answers, what do I do now? You've given me what amounts to about nine months to show improvement. What could I possibly do in that time?"

"Well, Fenton, nine months is better than the 90 days others in the bank wanted to give you. Count your blessings. Now if you really want my advice I have a suggestion that I think is your best hope."

Fenton didn't reply.

"I have to tell you honestly, Fenton. Most businesses don't recover from a warning like the one you got with the limited time you've been given. You really need to decide if it's worth it to you. Do you want it that bad? If the answer is yes, there is only one person I know who can help you make this turnaround, and that's Hugh Belden. Think about it and call me back if you decide your business is worth it. I will connect you with Hugh if you want me to. Fenton, the obstacles don't have to stop you."

Fenton gently hung up the telephone and just sat at his desk with his head in his hands.

CHAPTER
3

THE DECISION

Is It Worth The Trouble?

His job hadn't been so bad. *They treated me O.K. and the pay was steady. I didn't have too much to worry about,* he thought. Things were vastly different now for Fenton Rice. He was 42 years old. Making the decision to leave his job and start his own marketing firm six years ago had seemed like the right thing to do at the time. Now he was not so sure. The six years he had been in business had been a roller coaster of emotions. He had experienced the scary but exhilarating feeling of leaving the perceived security of his job. But he had also had to deal with the stress of not being able to pay the bills.

Either way, he was proud of being called an entrepreneur. He wasn't sure what the term really meant, but he knew people thought highly of him and respected what he had done with the business.

Although he liked the praise he got from others, it too was a part of Fenton's frustration.

Everyone thinks I am doing well, and I'm not. He was upset that he had let things get this bad but was not surprised. The letter from the bank just confirmed what he already knew. He was in trouble and now the bank was involved. Everything was at risk and they had only given him nine months to turn things around.

How did I let this happen? he thought.

The company had drifted further and further away from what it was supposed to be. Their financial performance was flat. There was little excitement inside the business. There was no attention to finding new ways to serve the customer.

But his company's performance was not Fenton's only concern. There was something else wrong. Something that he could not put his finger on. It just didn't feel right. It was tougher and tougher to come to the office everyday and to do the things he needed to do.

He knew the employees had to have noticed that things weren't right. They hadn't said anything, but he could tell they had been talking among themselves. Something had to change, and it had to change quickly. What was Fenton going to do?

He clearly had a decision to make. Growing up, he had seen many black business owners fail and blame the system, and especially the bank. Is this what they meant? Was the system about to get him? Or was Carol right that race was just an obstacle he would have to deal with?

If I give up now it means I've failed. I can do this. I know I can. Even if the system is against me, I can run a successful business.

He picked up the telephone and dialed Carol's number.

"I only have nine months" he said aloud as he waited for her to answer. "The end of the year! What can I do in nine months?" He had no idea, but he knew he had to figure it out. Meeting with this guy Hugh might be a good first step.

"This is Carol," the voice on the telephone answered.

"Carol, this is Fenton. I would like to meet with your friend Hugh. Can you give me his number?"

"Hugh doesn't work that way, Fenton. I will contact him for you and set up the meeting."

Fenton thought all of the drama about Hugh was a little strange but he was in no position to ask a lot of questions. "Fine. Let me know where we're going to meet."

*"I don't know what to do.
I have more questions
than answers."*

CHAPTER 4

THE PARK

Can This Guy Really Help?

Fenton wondered why Hugh wanted to meet with him in the park. Before his entrepreneurial days Fenton used to spend time sitting in Monument Park just three blocks from his home. The park always calmed him and helped clear his head. He hadn't had time for that since he started this business. Fenton missed the park, but now he was on his way there to hear why his business was not successful. *That's a great way to ruin a trip to the park*, he thought.

Before he knew it he was in the park and approaching 'his' bench. He didn't remember the walk but it did feel good to be back in the park. He noticed an old man sitting on the bench. *That couldn't be Hugh.*

Fenton sat down. He could not help but notice the old man's appearance. He looked like he was about 100 years old. He was a small black man, well dressed, but not elaborate. He wore a rain coat and a "gentleman's hat" much like the one

Fenton remembered his grandfather wearing. His face was full of deep wrinkles but still handsome. He looked a well defined combination of wise, tough and worn. The old man said nothing as Fenton sat down.

After a few moments Fenton leaned forward, looking at the old man and said "Good morning. My name is Fenton Rice."

"Good morning, Fenton. My name is Hugh Belden." The old man went on, "I come to this park and this bench every Friday morning. It is my time to reflect on my life and the lessons I have learned."

"I used to come here often myself," replied Fenton "until I started my own business. I just don't have the time anymore."

Hugh didn't speak. He just nodded his head in agreement.

The two men were silent again.

"Carol tells me you're in a tight spot, Fenton. How can I help?"

"This all started with the letter from the bank. Did Carol tell you about it?"

"Yes she did."

"I don't know what to do. I have more questions than answers. What do I do in response to the letter? What is wrong with my business? I have done everything I was supposed to. I wrote a business plan, went to training courses, and even invited in consultants to help me improve performance." Just talking about the whole situation was beginning to make Fenton angry all over again.

He recalled all of the statistics he had seen, the stories he had read and the conversations he had shared with other black business owners.

Fenton reached into his breast pocket and pulled out a report on entrepreneurs he had been reviewing and handed it to Hugh. "The message of this report is clear. The profile of the typical entrepreneur is a white male, a child of entrepreneurial parents, over $100,000 net worth, and the list of common attributes goes on. I don't have any of those attributes."

He was right. None of the report seemed to reflect Fenton's situation. "With all of the obstacles, why am I even still trying?" The more he thought about his situation the more frustrated he became. "It's the system," Fenton said aloud.

"If you are asking about the obstacles, you are asking the wrong question."

CHAPTER
5

THE QUESTION
Am I Asking The Right Question?

"The system will not let me succeed." The attitude of the bank was just one more example of that. "They're holding me back." Fenton stated angrily.

Hugh paused for a moment as if he were literally searching his mature mind for just the right words.

"Have you ever considered that you may be asking the wrong question, young man?"

"What question are you talking about?" Fenton asked.

"Fenton, everything you just said is exactly right. But all of those facts only matter if you are asking, 'why aren't black businesses more successful?' Tell me, Fenton, if you knew the answer to that question what good would it do you? What actions would you take? What things would you change?"

Fenton just listened. "Hugh, are you saying race is not the obstacle? That the system is not against me?"

"No, I am not saying that at all. But I am saying that whatever the obstacle, it is not what matters most. If you are asking about the obstacles, you are asking the wrong question."

"Think for a moment, Fenton," Hugh continued. "Do you know any successful businesses owned and operated by blacks?"

Fenton was starting to feel a little like a 7th grader getting too many questions and not having the right answers.

Who is this old man?, Fenton thought. *He hasn't even asked what type of business I own, and he is already beginning to drill me with questions. What does he know? He is obviously too old to understand the complexities of today's business world.*

Fenton put aside his thoughts, collected himself and politely replied, "Of course there are successful black owned businesses."

"Then tell me, what about those business owners allows them to be successful despite the obstacles that you say are so commonly discussed? How are they successful?"

Fenton did not have an immediate response.

Hugh continued, "Let me tell you what it's not. It has little to do with education, marital status, and even economic background. Not that those factors don't matter at all, but they're just not the things that make the ultimate difference. What makes them successful has little to do with who their parents are, how much money they had to get started, and even how great the business idea."

Hugh stopped talking as if he had finished his thought. He reached into the small brown paper bag on his lap to grab a handful of seed that he threw toward the birds.

Fenton was now firmly caught in the middle of being almost offended by the old man and really wanting to know more about what he was saying.

Hugh was still quietly watching the birds eat the newly thrown seed. Fenton wondered if that was all Hugh was planning to say.

After a few moments Fenton posed the question. "If none of those things are the reasons for their success, what is?"

Still Hugh said nothing. He grabbed another handful of bird seed. A few moments of silence passed. Fenton was thinking that the quiet was actually pretty nice. He hadn't had much time to think lately. Sitting in the park, he could hear the birds chirping. He could feel himself getting more and more relaxed. The problems of his business seemed far away from this peaceful spot in Monument Park.

He really did want to know what Hugh had to say about the success of entrepreneurs, but he was not going to ask again.

Hugh cleared his voice to speak, "Fenton, I have found through the years that at times the more I talk the less I'm heard. Sometimes you have to just wait until a person is ready to hear you."

He paused again and tossed the seeds he had been holding.

"Are you ready?" he said.

"Ready for what, Hugh?"

"Ready to hear how some business owners are successful despite the obstacles."

"Yes, I am," Fenton replied.

"You want to be sure you're ready because what I have to tell you will be different from anything you have ever been taught in business development programs, and maybe even contrary to what you read about business success in popular magazines. Some of it will challenge your own current thinking and may invite you to consider things that will make you uncomfortable. Are you open to that?"

Fenton thought he was ready to hear what Hugh had to say. The way Hugh was talking now made him wonder. Despite his reservations, he responded positively. "Trust me, Hugh, I'm ready to really listen."

CHAPTER
6

THE REALITY

Can You Handle The Truth?

"Fenton, there are three things that I want you to understand before you can understand anything else. These three things will never block your success or hurt your business, unless, of course, you fail to remember them."

Fenton nervously readjusted his position on the bench.

"I call them Sobering Realities because they are the opposite of what most of us wish were true."

"O.K." Fenton said.

"First is a reality that there will always be those who will succeed because of privilege. Always! Rest assured they will be the exception and not the rule, but they will always exist. Being angry about their success will not change their situation, but may kill your opportunity. Who cares if they are successful? Their success does not stop yours."

29

Hugh went on, "If we were honest, we would all admit that we hope to leave our children in a 'privileged' situation too. Dwelling on the privileged is a waste of time and energy. Do you understand what I mean?"

"I have never really thought about it, but yes, I think I get it." Fenton replied.

Hugh continued, "Second, entrepreneurship is not a movement. Entrepreneurs are individuals and the pursuit of entrepreneurship is an individual exercise. If you wait for a movement, you could be waiting forever. Movements may have been an effective way to change social issues, but in entrepreneurship, you have to be ready to push out on your own."

Fenton looked puzzled. "Do you mean I should not try to get help or partner with others?"

"No! That's not what I mean. Getting help and forming alliances is a great way to build your business. What I am saying is that if you get no help and find no one to align with, it will have to be O.K. with you. You have to be ready to keep going.... on your own. Does that make it more clear?"

Fenton was still processing what Hugh was saying. It all made sense, but didn't feel so good. He recognized some of what Hugh was pointing out in his own behavior. Trying to connect with others was one of the major sources of Fenton's disappointment.

"That is a tough one to hear, Hugh," Fenton admitted.

"I warned you that this may be hard on you," Hugh reminded. "It's natural to want some company."

People had begun to come to the park. Fenton was not sure how long he and Hugh had been there, but he didn't want to look at his watch and make Hugh think he was concerned about the time. He could hear the children playing and dogs barking around them.

"Hugh, is this new thinking going to change my business? Is changing my thinking going to make me successful?"

"I am confident it will change your business. I can't answer whether it will make you more successful," Hugh replied.

Fenton was surprised. "Success is what it's all about. If you don't know it will make me more successful, then what's the point?"

"I don't know because I don't know what your success is, Fenton."

"Hugh, my success is just like everyone else's."

"And what's that?"

"What do you mean, 'what's that?' I want to be a success like other people are. We all measure success the same way."

"How is that, Fenton?" pressed Hugh.

"The size of my business, the number of people I employ,

and the amount of money I can donate to causes. Things like that."

"Go on, Fenton. What else?"

"Well, of course, how much money I make and the things I am able to buy."

"You're right. Just about everyone does see success the same way, and that is the biggest problem with success. So you think if you have a large business and make a lot of money, that you will be happy with your success?" asked Hugh.

Fenton thought it might be a trick question. He pondered it for moment and then answered, "Yes. I do."

"You might be right. Maybe you would be very happy. And maybe you wouldn't. Folks have gotten successful entrepreneurship all screwed up. That's the third Sobering Reality."

"What is, Hugh?"

"That entrepreneurship is not freedom to do whatever you want. The real freedom and the success of entrepreneurship is in your ability to want whatever you want."

"What do you mean?"

"Fenton, tell me, what frustrates you most about your business right now?" Hugh asked.

"What?"

"You have said that you are frustrated. I am wondering what frustrates you?" Hugh clarified.

It was a good question. What was so frustrating? "It's probably the growing complexity of the business." Fenton replied.

"What do you mean?" Hugh questioned.

"Well, the larger we grow, the more complex our banking relationships. The more people we have, the more complex the management issues."

As Fenton spoke the words, Hugh's point was becoming clear. Fenton had always thought success meant more, and maybe it didn't.

"Hugh, are you suggesting that I want less?" asked Fenton.

"Of course not. But I am suggesting that you know what you want."

"O.K., I get it," Fenton said.

"What do you get?" asked Hugh.

"We have to define our own success." said Fenton.

"Good, but it goes a step further than that, Fenton. Part of the motivation for entrepreneurship is the freedom it can create. If someone else is telling you what success is, how much different is that from any job?"

NEW THINKING

A. Why business owners fail =
   wrong question.
   How they succeed =
   right question.

B. Three Sobering Realities.

   1. There will always
      be those of privilege.

   2. Entrepreneurship
      is not a movement.

   3. Entrepreneurial Success =
      The Freedom to decide
      what success is.

Fenton, just looked into space. He had heard every word that Hugh said but now he was confused about what he really wanted. He was so used to wanting what "everyone" said he should.

"Fenton, if you expect to get different results, you must be willing to think differently about everything you once thought was right."

So many thoughts were going through Fenton's mind. Hugh had said a great deal with his Sobering Realities. Fenton was not sure how to fit them all into himself and his business, but it didn't feel like it was the right time to ask. He just sat there silently thinking. The park really was a great place to think.

*   *   *   *   *

"Meet me here next Friday and we'll talk more, Fenton. In the meantime look up the word 'principle' in the dictionary. You will need to understand the definition to begin to understand the success of the entrepreneur."

Hugh began the process of rising from the park bench. After some effort, he made it to his feet. He paused a moment to look at Fenton. "Be sure to bring that definition."

Hugh shuffled off down the park sidewalk.

Fenton was thinking hard as he walked away from the park. This was not what he had expected when Carol said Hugh would help. He thought he would simply tell him what to do, but Fenton was willing to be patient for now.

35

Hugh did have a lot of good stuff to say and Fenton didn't want to lose any of it. When he returned to his office he decided to keep notes from each conversation. He wrote "New Thinking" and then: A. Why business owners fail = wrong question. How they succeed = right question. B. Three Sobering Realities. 1. There will always be those of privilege. 2. Entrepreneurship is not a movement. 3. Entrepreneurial Success = The freedom to decide what success is.

He slipped the note under the clear plastic mat in the middle of his desk so that it would stay in his sight.

CHAPTER
7

THE SET-UP

What's Inside Your Circle?

Friday morning came quickly. Fenton rose early as usual.

He approached the park bench where he had met Hugh before. Hugh was already there with a bag of seeds, feeding the birds. Fenton sat down. "Morning, Hugh."

"Morning, Fenton. The birds seem more anxious than usual today."

Fenton hadn't noticed the birds' behavior but he did take a moment to look.

Hugh continued, "They are here every day waiting for people to feed them. As long as we do, they will probably never even consider getting food on their own."

He reached into his small paper bag and threw the seeds in front of them.

"I guess it does take some effort to at least bend down to pick up the seeds," Hugh concluded.

Fenton was not sure where Hugh was going with the conversation. He remained silent for a moment and then spoke, "I have the definition."

"Good. Give it to me."

"The dictionary had many definitions, and I wasn't sure which one you wanted." explained Fenton.

"What do you mean, 'which one I wanted'?" asked Hugh.

"You asked me to get the definition of principle," Fenton replied. "I was just not clear which one you wanted me to get."

Hugh looked straight ahead. "Fenton, you're a bright guy. Based on our previous conversation, I'm going to bet you found one that meant something to you."

"Well, yes I did. But...," Fenton started.

"No buts," Hugh interrupted, "the definition I want to hear is the one that makes sense to you. Tell me about that definition, Fenton."

Fenton reached into his jacket pocket and pulled out a piece of paper. He felt a little nervous. What if the definition he chose wasn't the one Hugh expected?

"Principle is a rule or code of conduct," Fenton blurted.

Hugh said nothing. It was as if he was expecting more. *That's all I have,* Fenton thought.

He continued, "Hugh, I am not sure I understand why this definition is so important."

"It's important because it is the element of entrepreneurship that rarely gets considered anymore. Let me try to make it simple, Fenton. Principles are something you live by, not something that you think. It's what people mean when they refer to 'gut feeling,' or when they say their heart told them to do something. Those things come from personal codes of conduct. They come from principles."

The men both looked ahead. Fenton was trying to put the pieces together in his mind, and Hugh seemed to be giving him the time to do just that.

"Most people think that success is based on how smart they are, how much they know." Hugh shook his head, "They've got it all wrong. The biggest contributor to our success is our ability to deal with obstacles. This whole thing is about overcoming obstacles and getting results. Your ability to do that is based on your ability to get what you need to get, to do what you need to do."

"What do I need to get?" Fenton asked.

"It depends" replied Hugh. "Sometimes you need to get patience. Other times you need to get knowledge. Still other

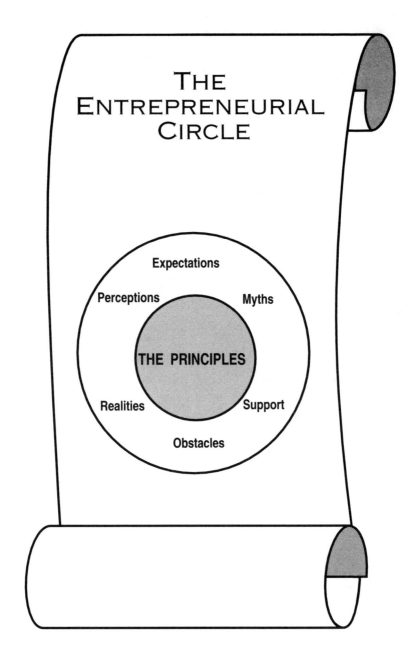

THE
ENTREPRENEURIAL
CIRCLE

Expectations

Perceptions

Myths

THE PRINCIPLES

Realities

Support

Obstacles

times you may need prayer. It depends on the obstacle you are facing."

"How do I know what I need?" asked Fenton.

"You may not 'know.' You may have to go with what you feel. But you decide based on principles."

Fenton listened intently, following each step of Hugh's explanation. He could feel that he was close to the crux of the blessing for which they had been working.

"Think of it this way." Hugh leaned over and picked up a stick that sat beneath the park bench. He drew two circles, one inside the other, in the patch of dirt between where the two men sat. "This outside circle is the world we live in. It is full of myths, realities, perceptions, expectations, support, and all of that, some of which are there to help us. Other things are only obstacles and some of it could be both. We really can't control what happens in this circle."

Fenton nodded his head to show he understood.

"This one is yours." Hugh said pointing to the smaller circle inside the larger one. "This is the world you have the opportunity to create. If you use the right principles, they allow you to let the good stuff into your circle and they help you push back on things that will not help you. This internal circle will determine how well you are able to overcome obstacles."

"So the principles are strategies to create this environment to get results?" Fenton questioned.

"You're close, Fenton. But I can't say that the principles are strategies, because strategies are driven by your thoughts. The principles are more like understandings that you discover you need."

"And then I get better results by living these principles?"

"Exactly, Fenton," Hugh nodded. "The principles create a world that allows the entrepreneur to overcome obstacles."

Fenton felt like he had been on a long journey. He thought hard about how important it was to overcome obstacles but he still was not sure about how the principles helped do that.

"Don't worry about completely understanding this idea right now. Give it some time. You'll understand better very soon," Hugh assured him.

CHAPTER
8

THE SUPPORT

What's Holding Me Up?

Hugh gave Fenton time to collect his thoughts. Time was no longer an issue. Fenton was completely engaged in understanding the principles. After a few moments, Hugh spoke.

"Young man, the first principle is about how you handle support."

"Support? What do you mean support?"

"Support comes in two flavors, Fenton. The first I call 'passive support.' This is the support that all entrepreneurs need but isn't directly related to the business. It's the support that often allows you to keep doing what needs to be done. This is the support that usually comes from family, friends, and even from a personal relationship with God."

"Can you give me some examples, Hugh?" Fenton asked.

"Sure! You've been in business a few years. Think of the times you have needed to ask your family to sacrifice something to allow you to do what you are doing."

Fenton could easily think of many of those occasions. But he had never before considered them as support.

Hugh went on, "Now think for a moment. What would your business life have been like if they had not agreed to support you?"

Fenton nodded and thought, *It would have been difficult to continue.* Then he said, "You also mentioned God. What did you mean by that?"

"Fenton, I'm a Christian; Baptist as a matter of fact, so I call my higher power God. No matter what you call him, or even her, I guess, many entrepreneurs believe they benefit from spiritual support."

"I'm not a very religious guy, Hugh," Fenton admitted.

"That's O.K. with me, Fenton. I am not here to save your soul, I'm here to challenge your thinking. I'll use me as the example to make you more comfortable. There are often issues, concerns, and even obstacles that I can only share with God. Having a place to share my issues lifts the burden from just being mine. It's not that obstacles just move out of my way, but it gives me the energy to do something about them."

Fenton was not sure what to say.

"Remember, the principles are meant to help you get what you need to get, to do what you need to do."

Fenton was now in deep thought. There had been times when Fenton felt he had no one he could talk to. He had often felt like he was carrying the burden of the business all by himself and that no one could understand his situation, but he was not sure that God was the answer for him.

"Fenton, most business owners don't fail, they quit. And they mostly quit because it is too tough to go on. That's why passive support is critical," Hugh said.

"The second type of support is 'active support,'" Hugh continued. "This is the support you hear most about. This is the support that gives you answers to direct questions."

"You mean things like training courses, financial support, and technical assistance?" Fenton asked.

"Exactly." Hugh replied. "And active support is also very important. You can get all of the knowledge you need if you are open to it. But alone, passive and active support would not really be a big deal. It is how well you 'accept' the support that really helps you get the results."

"When you say 'accept,' do you mean how often I use them?" Fenton asked.

"Not just how often, but how well you use them. How well do you let them into the circle? Do you give your family enough information to support you? Do you respect their needs in the whole process? When you come back from a seminar, do you actually implement the ideas or do you never get around to it? When you buy new software to help your business, do you actually install and use it? Do you seek out good advice and listen to it when you get it? Do you surround yourself with people who may be supportive, but critical of what you are doing or do you only want to hear from people who agree with you?"

It was as though Hugh knew his exact situation. Fenton had more support than he realized, but had not done a good job of accepting the support. And, as for prayer, anything past the blessing at the dinner table rarely happened.

"Hugh, I have a decent network of support, but I have not done a good job of really making it a part of my business."

"That's O.K., Fenton. Many haven't."

"How can I improve?" Fenton asked.

"You already have."

Puzzled, Fenton asked, "What do you mean?"

"You improve when you discover that this is a Principle you want to live," Hugh replied. "You improved the second day we got together. It was that day you decided to accept my support."

"It sounds too simple," said Fenton.

"It is simple," Hugh explained. "It's so simple that people often live right through it. You know you need support but do you think about what it takes to accept it? What good is support if you don't use it?"

Hugh reached into his pocket and passed Fenton a neatly folded piece of paper. "Think about these questions between now and our next meeting. The questions will help you figure out how you are doing with your support."

Hugh was already making his move to leave. "Fenton, Let's meet again in a month. I hope to see you."

Fenton didn't respond. He was already busy reviewing the questions Hugh had given him.

*   *   *   *   *

Fenton's trip back to the office was a blur. His thoughts were completely focused on his conversation with Hugh.

He read the questions aloud for the fourth or fifth time. "Who is a part of my *passive* support? Who is a part of my *active* support? Does my active support meet the criteria that allows them to really help? (Will tell me the truth, have the needed knowledge, care about my success and are not TOO impressed by me.) Do I have an ongoing way to communicate with each group?"

Fenton grabbed another piece of paper and began to write the questions and his answers to them. When he was done, he reviewed what had become his plan to both get and accept support.

47

QUESTIONS OF SUPPORT

1. Who is a part of my passive support?

2. Who is a part of my active support?

3. Does my active support meet the criteria that allows them to really help?
   - Will tell me the truth
   - Have needed knowledge
   - Care about my success
   - Are not TOO impressed by me

4. Do I have an ongoing way to communicate with each group?

My biggest source of passive support is my wife and children. I know it has to be hard for them because I don't often tell them what is going on or what they should expect he thought. *I have to do better if I expect their support.* Weekly meetings with the family was the first step of his plan and that part would start tonight.

Creating the list of active supporters was more difficult. Fenton had not really spent much time listening to people. After some thought he came up with four names. Two were business owners in other types of business, one was a banker he had met through a leadership program and stayed in contact with and the fourth worked as a middle level manager in a large corporation. They all met the criteria.

First he picked up the telephone and called his wife. He wanted to tell her about the family meeting he wanted to have that night. "I'll pick up some fried fish from the fish house for dinner," he said.

Then he called the four people on his advisory group list. He told them about what he was planning to do and why he was asking for their help. He made it clear that for the next nine months he wanted to meet every month, but expected to meet only once a quarter thereafter. Three of them said they would be glad to help. The fourth was more reluctant, and Fenton accepted her position as a no, at least for now. The first meeting was scheduled for early Monday morning.

Fenton felt better already. He felt like he was doing something and that these steps were really going to make a difference.

The next few weeks went by quickly. Fenton was busy meeting with his advisory group and moving forward on some of the ideas and suggestions they provided. He felt a renewed energy, and almost a sense of freedom from the fact that his family really knew what was going on.

It was Thursday afternoon and Fenton was busy completing his preparation for the next day's meeting with Hugh. He was ready.

CHAPTER
9

THE VALUE

Why Am I Really In Business?

Hugh was again already on the park bench when Fenton arrived. The two men exchanged greetings. Fenton wanted to tell Hugh about the weekly meetings he had planned with his family and the monthly meetings with the advisory group, but Hugh went straight into asking Fenton questions.

"Fenton, if you could give me only two reasons why your business exists, what would they be?"

Fenton wondered what this had to do with his current situation.

"Just two?" said Fenton looking up into the air to find his thoughts. "I would probably say to make money and to have freedom from an employer, but what does that have to do with what is going on?"

"It has to do with the second principle and it's interesting that you said nothing about what your business does."

"What do you mean? You asked me for two reasons for my business to exist. I just answered your question."

"You're right, Fenton. I did ask the question, but how you answered it says a lot about what you think about your business."

"I am not sure I understand."

"The answers you gave focused on what you get, versus what you give."

It was clear that Fenton was not getting it. Hugh patiently went on, "Maybe a few examples will make it more clear. Jewelry designers give beautiful jewelry. Professional speakers give challenge, information and inspiration to audiences. Accountants give accurate information and advice to clients. Clothing retailers give attractive clothing."

Fenton just listened.

"The fact that they make money and have freedom and all of the other things that come from being entrepreneurs, is because they do what it is their business does. They understand that the reason for the business is to deliver some value. They focus on giving value and profit is the outcome."

"Are you trying to convince me that I shouldn't care about making money?" asked Fenton.

"Of course not, Fenton. That would be ridiculous. But what I am saying is that you shouldn't 'focus' on making money."

It was another one of those moments when Fenton had to remind himself of the warning Hugh had given about challenging everything he thought was right about business. But how would this work? How could he run a successful business and not focus on the money?

"Hugh, I have to focus on the money."

"You don't have to. You choose to, based on your understanding of what you think will make you successful," Hugh replied. "Of course you have to control your spending, be sure your product is priced correctly and keep your eye on your budget."

"Isn't that focusing on money?" Fenton asked.

"No, it's not — that's managing the money," said Hugh. "The danger is that the numbers become the business. The value you give must drive the numbers, not the other way around. The business must have a purpose and giving value must be a part of it."

"Hugh, why is this so important?"

"It is important because you wanted to understand how successful entrepreneurs do it; how they overcome obstacles. Focusing on the value the business gives is a big part of their success," Hugh replied.

"What is it about focusing on value that helps them be successful?" Fenton questioned.

"Your actions follow your focus, Fenton. When you move your focus away from the value the business gives, you move your actions away too."

"What happens then?" Fenton asked.

"That's when bad things start. Quality declines, customer service diminishes, and ultimately you don't make money. Your business is suffering right now from a focus on what you get. If you focus on the value you give, the money will come, and it will come because of that value. You get the picture?"

"Yeah, I do," said Fenton. He had allowed his focus to shift.

Hugh went on, "We have already talked about the ups and downs of entrepreneurship. Do you remember that?"

"Of course I do," said Fenton

"Then tell me, Fenton, what do you have to hang on to when the money is not as good as you hoped? What do you focus on when you can't get in to see the client that you think will change your whole business? What do you think about when you face a major obstacle?"

The two men were silent. Fenton didn't answer. He was carefully pondering each of the questions and Hugh was giving him time to think.

"Fenton, I'll tell you what you focus on. You focus on the value you add to the customers that you serve. Why? Because that's sometimes all you've got. Focusing on anything else makes those rough spots rougher, and makes it more difficult to recover. Focus on the value you give, Fenton, and the profit will come."

Fenton still had questions. "How do you keep your eye on the money, but not get distracted by it?"

"Some of this you will have to work out on your own. I suggest the first step would be writing out the answer to the question, What value do you give? Make sure everyone involved knows it and understands its importance. And then never make a decision that hurts that purpose."

"It just seems tough to do," Fenton admitted.

"Your thinking too much. Just let yourself feel what I am talking about. You're right, focusing on value is tough to do, but it's what it takes to overcome many of the obstacles that are in your way. It's a new way of thinking and new thinking is never easy."

Fenton knew Hugh was right again. He remembered back to when he started the business. There was no money. There was no status. All he had was the value he gave his clients and that was what he enjoyed the most.

How had he gotten off track? *I guess it doesn't matter*, he thought. He had to find a way to focus on the value to the client again.

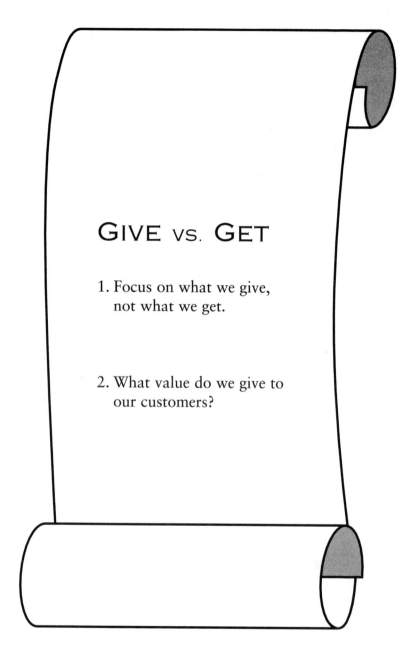

GIVE vs. GET

1. Focus on what we give, not what we get.

2. What value do we give to our customers?

Hugh sighed aloud, "Well, Fenton, our time together is coming to an end."

Fenton hadn't even considered the time until that moment.

"The next Principle is serious and trust me, you have heard this one before. Right now I think it's best we take a break. Let's do this again next month."

Fenton really didn't want to wait that long. He was feeling the pressure of needing to make immediate changes in his business, but Hugh was already making his way down the sidewalk. The conversation was over for now. He would have to wait.

*   *   *   *   *

Fenton sat in his office pondering the value his business gives. He had been focused on making money for so long, it was really hard to think clearly about anything else. He pulled out a piece of paper and wrote "Give vs. Get" 1) Focus on what we give, not what we get. 2) What value do we give to our customers? He wrote down three or four ideas. He ran the ideas by others in his company. They had a lot of input and really improved on what Fenton was thinking. When they were finished, Fenton had the company's value statement made into a sign and posted it on the wall in the office.

We make our clients more profitable by providing innovative marketing solutions that are always on time and within budget.

But he remembered that Hugh said that talking about value was only window dressing if you didn't have a business that really lived to give that value. Fenton called a company meeting and talked to everyone about the value the company gives. Next came the tough work of finding anything and everything that distracted them from delivering that value. They looked at rules, procedures and even marketing strategies that led their activities away from the value they give. Everything was considered for change.

CHAPTER
10

THE CRISIS

We Were Making Progress, Now What?

The ring of his telephone caught him off guard. It was Carol from the bank. After the brief greetings, Fenton rolled straight into explaining how things were going with Hugh. "He is great, Carol. We have just begun to talk about the principles, but already his advice has changed my approach to getting and accepting support and refocusing on the value we give to our clients. I have formed an advisory group that will help me make better decisions and ..."

Carol interrupted, "That's great, Fenton. It is good to hear your work with Hugh is progressing. But I'm calling with bad news."

Fenton's heart sank. *What could it be now?*

"Fenton, you guys just aren't keeping up. Not only are you behind on your loan payments, but your line of credit is at the maximum. To make matters even worse, your checking account is overdrawn. The bank hates to see that, Fenton. With all of your other issues, you don't need to have an overdrawn checking account."

Fenton was silent. Just when he thought he was putting things in order.

"I know how much the last letter bothered you. I wanted to call you before you got another one. Bob could be in his office writing another letter right now."

"Carol, tell me straight. Am I out of time?"

"I am not sure, Fenton, but if I were you I would plan as though I were."

"What can I do?"

"Fenton, I suggest you talk it through with Hugh."

"But we're not scheduled to get together until the end of the month."

"I will contact him for you now and set up a meeting."

"Thanks Carol."

Fenton hung up the telephone. He was surprised by how he felt about Carol's news. He was not angry. He felt more numb than anything. It was almost as though this whole thing were happening to someone else. He had no idea what to do. He mostly felt like quitting. He could not even imagine what life beyond this crisis might look like. He sat for a moment thinking about nothing at all. He just sat.

Carol called back in just a few minutes and confirmed a meeting with Hugh for that afternoon.

*   *   *   *   *

The park was much busier in the afternoon than during their early morning meetings. Hugh was waiting.

Fenton sat down with a huge sigh. He was obviously frustrated to a point of panic and fatigue by this time. He told Hugh about the latest conversation with Carol. Hugh sat patiently nodding from time to time to be sure Fenton knew he was listening.

"So what can I do, Hugh? How do we fix this one?"

"The short answer is, you stay the course. There are four principles that create success. We've only talked about two of them."

"Hugh, were you listening? I don't have time for that," Fenton shouted.

"Then you should quit, Fenton because this is all there is. No other course gets you there. You said you wanted success. Do you?"

"Of course I do, but..."

"Do you want it badly enough?"

Fenton hesitated. "I'm tired, Hugh. I've been at it too long and I have too little to show for it."

All Fenton could think about now was failing. Many of his friends had nine-to-five jobs and were doing just fine. They didn't have the headaches and stress Fenton dealt with everyday.

"Decide, Fenton! This is the moment. You can quit right now. Your situation can't get any worse. Are you in or out? Decide because I can't help you until you do."

"It's worth it, but it's tough", Fenton replied. "But don't worry, I'm in."

"Then we never have this conversation about quitting again. Quitting is no longer an option. Agreed?"

"Agreed."

"Hugh, the reality is that time is short. What do I do right now?"

"You haven't gotten any written communication from the bank yet, have you?"

"No."

"Good. You have to contact them before they contact you. Call them now and ask for a meeting with Carol and her boss Bob in the next seven days. Tell them you want to present your comprehensive plan to turn around your business."

"Hugh, what comprehensive plan?"

"Fenton, you have already started to put the plan together. Carol mentioned your advisory group. Good idea! We just have to work through the rest of the principles. Make the call to the bank. I will see you back here in the morning."

Fenton thought for a moment. Hugh was right. Once you take quitting off the table, the next moves become much more clear. He pulled out his telephone and called the bank to set up the meeting.

"It just doesn't seem fair but it is as fair as it is."

CHAPTER
11

THE WEAPON

Am I Good Enough To Compete?

Fenton flipped up the collar on his jacket to cover his ears. He was early. He thought it would be nice to beat Hugh to the park. The three block walk was cool this morning and the park seemed unusually quiet.

There was Hugh, waiting on the bench. *What's up with this guy?* Fenton thought. *Not matter how early I come he's already here. Does he live in the park?* Hugh spoke as Fenton began to take his seat next to him. "Fenton, our first conversation started with your complaints about the obstacles you face."

Hugh paused to collect his thoughts. He seemed to be placing the next few words in just the right order.

Before Hugh could continue his statement, Fenton jumped in. "It's a fact that black owned businesses are not treated equally in the market place. Maybe it's racism, maybe it's just perception and maybe the two are the same thing. However you define it, things are different for business owners like me."

Hugh leaned back slowly and paused. "Fenton, I understand what you're saying. Sounds just like how life was for black people when I was young. It has always baffled me that we have had a problem so long, and we still haven't figured out a solution."

Fenton replied with subtle irritation. "We have come up with solutions. We have set-aside programs, special funding sources, mentoring relationships and things like that."

Hugh now looked confused. "Then why aren't those programs working?"

"What's your point, Hugh? Are you suggesting we end special programs?"

"Fenton, I am not suggesting they go away but I do wonder why they have not made the playing field absolutely equal," Hugh clarified.

"Hugh, I am not sure that complete equality is possible."

"Now we agree, Fenton. I don't think complete equality is possible either...for anyone. Situations are just not going to be the same. The challenge is not to let the obstacles get in your head and take over."

"But the obstacles just seem so big, Hugh."

"So what do you do, Fenton?" Hugh was challenging Fenton now.

"What do you mean 'what do I do'? I keep fighting," Fenton replied.

"Right! But I suggest you start fighting with a different weapon."

"Weapon? That's a strong word, Hugh."

"You're right. It is a strong word, but I intended it to be. You are in a war, Fenton, and you have been battling your obstacles with the equivalent of rocks and sticks."

Hugh's tone surprised Fenton. He had not heard Hugh talk this way before. Weapons, wars and battles? His whole demeanor had suddenly gotten intense.

Hugh went on, "There is a secret weapon that works every time. Successful entrepreneurs understand that it's the only way to become successful and stay that way."

"What's that, Hugh?

"Excellence!" said Hugh, as if he had just uncovered a hidden jewel.

"Excellence? That's not new, Hugh."

"I told you you'd heard it before. It isn't new, but it is still rare and many of the very programs you say are working to level the playing field could also be working against excellence."

Fenton didn't like what Hugh was saying. No one should speak out against special programs. Even if they are flawed, they are better than nothing at all.

Hugh continued, "Fenton, I am too old to worry about the politics of what I am saying. I will leave that to you young folks to figure out. You asked what would help you overcome obstacles and have entrepreneurial success. Part of the answer is excellence."

"Hugh, even if you are excellent at what you do, the system will still hold you down."

"Don't be naive, Fenton. Think about what you're saying. Do you really believe that if you're the absolute, undisputed best at what you do, that people will not do business with you because you're black? No obstacle is that big. Only an idiot would take that approach, and you shouldn't want to do business with them anyway."

"Even if you are right, Hugh, everyone doesn't have to be that good to be successful. They get business anyway."

"I am not sure who 'they' are, and you could be right. But you're not everyone. Do I have to remind you about the Sobering Realities? You wanted to know what it takes to be successful. The greatest weapon you have is excellence."

"It just doesn't seem fair," Fenton said sadly.

"It is as fair as it is, Fenton."

Fenton was clearly frustrated with Hugh. He didn't like what he was hearing and he resented Hugh for saying it. But none of it was new. He had thought the same things himself. He had just never said or heard them aloud. They were cutting. *It's just not fair*, he thought. *Why do I have to be better to be successful?* He realized his thoughts were a waste of energy. Hugh struck a tender spot because Fenton knew that he had allowed the special programs to make him lazy. He knew his business was no longer pursuing excellence and he also knew what had to be done.

The two men just sat on the bench in Monument Park thinking. The park really was a great place to think.

"Define your own success and stay close to it."

CHAPTER
12

THE MOTIVATION

What Makes Me Keep Doing This?

Hugh finally broke the silence. "Fenton, I have given you almost all that I've got."

"What do you mean 'almost'?"

"There is just one more principle that may come in handy from time to time. I saved it for last, because although it is vitally important, it's also very hard to help people understand."

"What is it, Hugh?"

"One of the biggest reasons a business fails is because of missed expectations. Entrepreneurs think things will happen bigger, better, easier and, maybe most of all, sooner, than they actually do. Some people can delay gratification for many years, and others can hardly wait a few months."

"So what is the difference?" asked Fenton.

"Fenton, the difference is the reason you choose to do this

versus the many other ways you could make a living. It's what keeps you going through the tough times, invested money, disappointment and even threatening letters from the bank. It's passion, Fenton. You do it because you have a passion for it. Passion is the only motivating factor you can count on."

"I am not sure I understand, Hugh."

"The logic is simple, Fenton. If you love doing what you do, you are more likely to keep doing it. Despite obstacles, set-backs and disappointments, if your short-term motivation is passion, your chances of success improve."

Fenton was silent, but thinking.

"Being in business for yourself is full of ups and downs," Hugh continued. "You can think of passion as the bridge that gets you from one peak to the next and over the valleys in between."

"I understand what passion does, but what do you mean by passion?" Fenton asked. "Are you saying that I have to love the business that I am in?"

"Passion could come from a love for the business that you're in, or from an enjoyment of the process of being in business. Some people just love the transactions, negotiations, and things like that. Others love whatever the business does."

"So which one is better?"

"Neither is better, Fenton, as long as the outcome is day-to-day passion. I caution you that many entrepreneurs start with great excitement and even passion, and then they let the business take over and steal the passion away. That is why knowing what success is for you is so important. You drive what the business does, not the other way around."

Fenton immediately saw himself in what Hugh was saying. He had given control of the direction of the business over to the business. He had stopped doing what he wanted to do. He was doing what the business asked of him. *No wonder it had been harder and harder to come to the office. I've lost my passion.*

"Hugh, how do I get the passion back?" Fenton asked.

"You're already on your way. Define your own success, young man, and stay close to it. And remember passion is a feeling."

There was a period of silence that seemed as though it lasted forever.

Hugh spoke next. "Fenton, I need to tell you that this is our last meeting. It's your turn now. Remember, don't try to 'think' any of these principles. You have to live them. They have to become a part of 'how' you are. With them, there are no obstacles you can't overcome."

"But what if I need to talk things over with you? What if I get confused?"

"You will get confused and frustrated and tired. It's all a part of the process. But you won't need me to help you. There will be others to help you along your path. I have gone as far as I can with you."

"What others?"

"You never know, Fenton. People just happen into your life. My last advice is, if you're ever in doubt, or things aren't going well, go through the principles."

"What do you mean, 'go through them,' Hugh?"

"Make sure you are living them. Make sure your day-to-day activities show that the four principles are really your 'code of conduct,' Fenton."

Hugh made his move to rise from the park bench. It took him longer than usual this time. Fenton considered reaching out to help him, but wasn't sure Hugh would appreciate it. Hugh finally straightened. His steps were slower than Fenton had seen before. As he shuffled away, he said quietly, "I have given you all I have, Fenton. How you live it is up to you."

The moment felt final. Fenton knew he would not be seeing Hugh again, but it was O.K. He did feel ready. "Thank you, Hugh Belden," Fenton said. "Thanks for everything."

Hugh never turned around. He just raised his hand and mumbled his parting advice, "Just remember the principles."

It is up to me, Fenton thought. *How am I going to live the principles?*

The journey with Hugh and Fenton was over, but Fenton's journey was just beginning. He had a few months left.

CHAPTER
13

THE TURN

Can We Do This?

Fenton now sat alone on the park bench, deep in thought about what he needed to do next. His focus was on turning his business around. In his excitement he had almost forgotten the meeting he had requested with the bank in just a few days. Things seemed so clear to him now. He really 'felt' what Hugh was saying about excellence. He was still not so sure about this passion stuff, but he was sure about what he needed to do. He called his office and planned another meeting for all employees for the next day. He spent the rest of the evening planning and rehearsing what he would say.

* * * * *

Fenton woke up early as he always did, but this morning was different. Fenton felt relieved and excited about the meeting they were about to have and the improvement in the business. The original letter from the bank didn't seem to matter nearly as much.

Everyone was waiting for him when he got to the office. He greeted them and wasted no time. "Ladies and gentlemen, you have all noticed the changes we've been making. Many of you have been a part of the discussions. The fact is, we're not done yet. There is one last challenge we have to take on."

Everyone was glued to Fenton's words.

"We've done all right for most of the last few years. We've done just 'all right' because we've been just all right. Well, all right isn't good enough anymore. We have to figure out a way to be excellent and that will mean a radical change in how we do business."

Fenton's speech was becoming emotional. He wasn't sure why but he could feel the tears streaming down his cheeks. He wanted to overcome the obstacles more than he ever had before and he really felt as though he knew how. Maybe this was what Hugh meant by passion. Whatever it was, he could see the same thing in the faces of everyone in the room.

"People have been treating our company as second-class. Maybe they still will, but starting today, they will also know that we are in pursuit of excellence. We only have one goal and that is to be the best there is at what we do. For that, they will respect us."

Fenton wiped his cheeks. He couldn't remember the last time he had cried. His eighteen-year-old daughter teased that she didn't think he had ever cried. Sure he had cried, but not often, and never in front of people. But he felt what he was saying and he knew what it was going to mean to the success of every person in the room.

Fenton collected himself and began to read from a typed paper he had in his hand.

"Our plan for excellence is simple. We are going to ask ourselves five simple questions.

Number one, what are the things that are most important to OUR clients? For example, service, product quality, or technical support. Those items our clients see as important become the things that we must deliver excellently.

Number two, how are we doing on each important item right now? We'll rate ourselves poor, good, or excellent.

Number three, what is the evidence of our performance? We may need to develop brief surveys, talk about examples, and even complaints to be sure we really know how we are doing.

Number four, does anyone do it better? If we are not the best at the things that are important to OUR clients, who is? We have to find them and then determine what we can learn from them.

Number five, how can we do it better? This final question is where we get to work. This is where we begin to show our clients, our competitors and ourselves how good we can really be."

Fenton looked up. "If we keep asking ourselves these five questions we will be the excellent company we want to be.

FIVE QUESTIONS TO EXCELLENCE

1. What things are most important to our clients?
   (Service, product quality, technical support, etc.)

2. How are we doing on each?
   (Poor? - Good? - Excellent?)

3. What is the evidence of our performance?
   (Surveys, examples, complaints, etc.)

4. Does anyone do it better?
   (What can we learn from them?)

5. How can we do it better?

The questions are simple, but the discipline to consistently ask and answer them will be difficult."

His eyes panned the room. He looked at every person. "I have a very critical meeting with our bank in just a few days. The changes we have made are what I will share with them, but this plan for the pursuit of excellence is key. I think we're up to it, but I need to know from you. Can we do this?"

People looked at each other as they nodded their approval.

"Good then. We start today to make our tomorrow what WE want it to be."

*"We will be the best
at what we do."*

CHAPTER
14

THE MEETING

Will Our Plan Be Good Enough?

Fenton stood in front of the mirror in his bedroom at home. His wife knew how nervous he was. There was not much she could think to say. The meeting with the bank was just hours away and everything was riding on it. He tightened his tie.

"Good luck, Honey. You know we're all with you. Go show'm what the Rices are made of."

Fenton smiled, kissed her, grabbed his briefcase and left. Having and accepting her support had really taken away much of the stress of the situation.

The thirty minute drive to the downtown office of the bank seemed to fly by. Fenton knew he was ready, but he still had those butterflies in his stomach. The feeling actually reminded him of when he played high school football. The few minutes right before the game were always the most

THE LOST ART OF ENTREPRENEURSHIP

difficult. Once the game started, he was always fine, and this game was about to start.

Carol came out to greet him in the lobby. "Fenton, I'm so glad you called them before they had the chance to call you. You'll be meeting with my boss, Bob Case, Roger from community banking and me. Are you ready?"

Fenton nodded his head. His mind shifted to Hugh's last words of advice. *Just remember the principles.*

Fenton began by explaining his company's current situation. He laid out his strategy to fix some of the most pressing problems which led to the checking account overdraft and the missed loan payments.

"We have to do a better job of pricing our services and collecting the money that is owed us."

He asked the bankers directly if the bank planned to give him a few weeks to allow some of the short-term plans to work. They looked at each other and gave a lukewarm response that amounted to a weak commitment.

Fenton then shifted to his long-term plans to 'significantly' change his business. "We, that is to say I, went to sleep at the wheel. It's time to bring things back. We've strengthened our firm in four critical areas that we believe will quickly begin to separate us from our competition."

The three bankers just listened. Fenton could see Carol fighting back a smile. He knew he had them. He went on to explain the advisory group, the re-clarification of the company's value to clients, and the plan to continuously pursue excellence and how all of this activity had led to a new level of excitement within the company.

"At the worst time in our company's history, we're all more excited than ever before. We call it passion and it is what motivates us," Fenton said proudly. His mention of passion even surprised him. *That is what Hugh meant by passion*, he thought.

Bob Case interrupted "Sounds like a great plan, Fenton, but we see a lot of people with good plans. Have the changes created any real results?"

"Great question, Bob, and I am glad you asked." Fenton was clearly on a roll now. "Although much of the change is less than three months old, we have already increased our profit margin by 15%, improved our collection rate by 22%, increased our billable hours by 20% and lowered our general and administrative expenses by 30%. All of these improvements came from ideas from the first meeting with the advisory group. We firmly believe that the best is yet to come."

Bob just nodded. Carol could hardly contain her satisfaction.

"Folks, there's no doubt we're in a tough spot right now, but we are showing improvement. Over the next few months we'll continue to distinguish ourselves and improve the value we deliver to our clients. We will be the best at what we do."

They agreed to give Fenton and his company a reprieve for now. The original letter still held true. They would review his situation at the end of the year, and he must 'deliver on the promises' he had made that day.

Carol walked with Fenton out into the lobby and down the hall.

"Fenton, that was outstanding. They were ready to shut you down and now they want to buy stock. I was very proud of you in there."

"Carol, I really have you to thank for all of this. You've been helping me since I brought my business to this bank. It was you that tipped me off to the most pressing problems in time for me to be proactive. And, of course, you connected me with Hugh. That guy is something else."

"Yeah, I have heard that before. He would tell you that you came up with all the answers yourself. He just supplied the questions. Based on your performance today, I am guessing he would be right. That was all you in there Fenton."

"Thanks Carol."

They shook hands and Fenton turned and walked away. *She is a good sister*, he thought.

CHAPTER 15

THE REFLECTION

Who Is Hugh Anyway?

Things were far from perfect, but Fenton was excited about his business again and his excitement had begun to show tangible results. It had been months since Fenton's last conversation with Hugh. He often wondered about the small old man who had given him so much. *It's Friday,* he thought as he finished getting ready for work. "I'm going to stop by the park on my way to the office," he said aloud to himself. He really wanted to see Hugh and tell him about his progress, but he didn't want to get his hopes up. Hugh had made it clear that they had had their last conversation.

Fenton briskly walked the three blocks to the park. As he approached 'their' bench he could see another man sitting. He was too broad a man to be Hugh. This man was a fair skinned, handsome, black man who appeared to be in his early 50's.

Fenton sat down and introduced himself, "Hi. I'm Fenton Rice."

"Hello, Fenton Rice, I'm Will. Will Webb."

"Will, do you come here often?"

"I used to a few years ago. I used to meet a friend here every Friday."

Fenton was surprised by the coincidence, but he let the man continue.

"I met him right after I started my own business. I had worked for a large company for almost 30 years. I had a real problem with self doubt about being an entrepreneur. It really became a major obstacle. Old Hugh really put me on the right track."

"Did you say the man's name was Hugh?"

"Yes, Hugh Belden" Will replied. "Do you know him?"

"Yes, we've met." Fenton didn't want to interrupt the man's story with his own experience with Hugh.

"I didn't know who he was at the time, but I found out later that he was one of the most successful entrepreneurs in the country of any race. He owned businesses dating back to the early 1900's. I've often wondered if our conversations would have been different, or if I would have gotten as much as I did, had I known how successful he was."

Fenton was starting to understand more about the history of the principles. These ideas were not new. They were actually very old. Hugh had used them for more than 70 years. Fenton said nothing. He wanted to hear more of what Will knew about Hugh.

Will continued, "He had the strangest approach to business. He demanded that I question just about everything I ever thought about how to succeed as an entrepreneur. His approach made a lot of sense, but I really had to be open to thinking differently."

"What kind of things did he teach you?" asked Fenton hoping to hear about the principles.

"He started by changing my understanding of successful entrepreneurship. He would say that you cannot understand success by just looking at 'who' is successful. You get your true lessons by looking more closely at 'how' they're successful. How do they approach the business? What personal principles do they live by?"

It was all so familiar to Fenton, but it felt good to hear the words again.

Will continued, "Hugh's principles were, at times, difficult for me to hear, but they've really made the difference for me. I say the principles so often that they're never far from my mind: getting and accepting support, focusing on the value you give, not what you get, using excellence as a weapon against obstacles and ..."

"and maybe most importantly, making passion the motivating factor," Fenton injected.

Will didn't look surprised. "I figured you knew Hugh better than you let on."

"Hugh challenged me to be successful, Will. His advice saved my business and the principles really do guide my thinking. I will never forget him."

The men sat on the bench silently. Each was thinking about the impact the four principles had on their businesses and on their lives.

Fenton spoke next, "Where is Hugh these days?"

Will shrugged his shoulders and shook his head at the same time. Neither of the men knew for sure.

"He is probably sitting on another park bench feeding another group of birds," Will said.

Both men sat back on the bench in Monument Park and smiled. The park really was a great place to think.

The End

THE FOUR PRINCIPLES OF THE LOST ART OF ENTREPRENEURSHIP

1. Get and Accept *support*

2. Focus on the *value* you give, not on what you get

3. Use *excellence* as your primary weapon

4. Make *passion* your motivating factor

"The principles work, not because they remove obstacles, but because they make them a part of the entrepreneurial process."

AFTERWORD

WHY THE PRINCIPLES WORK

For many years, researchers and business experts have focused on 'who' entrepreneurs are. We have been looking for the differences in their backgrounds, education, parental influence, income level and even their race. This area of research provides us with very good demographic data and the ability to compare one entrepreneur to another. The principles from *The Lost Art Of Entrepreneurship* work, and they work absolutely because they focus on 'how' the entrepreneur is who they are. A focus on the principles transcends race, gender and any other obstacles. The difference may seem subtle, but is significant in explaining the effect of the principles on an entrepreneur's success.

We have been looking for what is different about the environment of a successful entrepreneur. The real key is that they create their own environment; their own inner circle. How else do we explain the many examples of entrepreneurs who have virtually none of the common characteristics for success, but are massively successful? The mystery is also present for those who seem to have everything they need, but repeatedly fail. The principles help to create an entrepreneurial environment, an inner circle, that encourages better use of resources, higher levels of satisfaction, increased levels of business quality, and improved longevity.

Living the principles makes the entrepreneur more proactive, more able to adapt to change and more prepared to recover from disappointment. Using the principles to build the entrepreneurial environment does not mean that the obstacles will go away. Common obstacles like lack of support, negative perceptions, misleading myths and even well meaning special programs are all a part of the general environment. These obstacles are just not allowed to become a part of the business.

Successful entrepreneurs 'battle' to keep the external elements from affecting 'how' they are. The principles work, not because they remove obstacles, but because they make them a part of the entrepreneurial process. The principles work because they become a part of 'how' the entrepreneurs live. They work because successful entrepreneurs understand that success can be the only outcome.

How The Principles Became A Story

Was he pushed or did he jump? A common question of "who done it" mysteries. When it comes to the development of this book, the truth is probably a little bit of both. I have written other books but all of my previous work has been in the conventional, non-fiction genre. The members of my Master Mind Group thought it was time that I really challenge myself and write in a different style. The purpose of the Master Mind Group is to help, challenge, and encourage the members to reach their individual objectives. The other members had enjoyed business books written in the form of fables and 'pushed' me to consider that approach. "That takes talent," I responded. I was hopeful that my humble position would cool them on the idea. They pressed on.

I had just completed new research in understanding the success of the entrepreneur, and I was pondering my next book. This seemed like a good time to give business fiction writing a chance. The outcome is *The Lost Art Of Entrepreneurship*. The content of the principles comes from in-depth interviews with successful entrepreneurs. The series of people I interviewed come together as the wise old man, Hugh, in the story. I trust you will agree that the business fiction genre was the perfect method for delivering the message of what successful entrepreneurs said made the difference for them. This story was just waiting to be told, and thanks to the little push from my Master Mind Group, the principles became a story. Thanks, Otis Williams, Jr. and Tammy Wynn.

Mel Gravely

ABOUT THE AUTHOR

MELVIN J. GRAVELY II, PH.D.

D r. Gravely is an entrepreneurial coach and the founder of the *Institute for Entrepreneurial Thinking*. He is also on the business faculty of *Thomas More College* and is the co-founder of *Infrastructure Services, Inc.* He is a member of the National Speakers Association and writes and speaks on various topics related to entrepreneurial thinking, small business development, marketing and leadership. He is also the author of three previous books, as well as many magazine and newspaper articles.

He has a BS in computer science from Mount Union College and an MBA from Kent State University. Dr. Gravely's Ph.D. is in Business Administration and Entrepreneurship from The Union Institute. He currently lives in Cincinnati with his family.

Find more information about
Mel Gravely on the web at:
www.melgravely.com

FREE AUDIO TAPE OFFER

Give us your feedback and we'll give you a FREE audio tape.

We want to hear from you. What did you think of *The Lost Art Of Entrepreneurship*? How did the book affect your business approach? Tell us about your success stories implementing the principles. Be sure to include your name and address and we will send you a FREE audio tape on, *The Lost Art Of Entrepreneurship*.

You can email us at:
info@entrethinking.com

or

Mail your comments to:
Institute For Entrepreneurial Thinking
Attn: The Lost Art
P.O. Box 621170
Cincinnati, Ohio 45262-1170